I Remembered Poetry

AF624585

Marie Williams

BookLeaf Publishing

Presentation by *BookLeaf Publishing*

Web: www.bookleafpub.com

E-mail: info@bookleafpub.com

ISBN: 9789357210553

First edition 2022

DEDICATION

Dedicated to every poet that found their pen.

I Write

I write for the mamas that can’t
the mamas that won’t
the mamas that don't
I write for the mamas that forget they have
voices
for the mamas who’s arms are too heavy to carry
the pen to the paper
who’s shoulders serve as the mantle to everyone
else’s world

for the mamas that gave up their dreams
for the mamas who’s story was chopped and
screwed
   skewed to project someone else’s view
for the mamas that forgot how to cry tears of joy
   because they’ve been crying tears of survival
for the mamas that protect their young with no
protection for themselves

I write -

for the woman evolved and reformed
   yet still hearing the stories of a past twice
removed
for the woman that wants to believe
   that age ain’t nothing but a number

but lives in fear of losing her memory
for the woman who's wrinkles tells stories
of a life lived several times over
but can't seem to find the silver lining in
the grays of her follicles
for the woman who's pride has her tongue tied
and unable to say "forgive me"
for the woman that's been saved by grace
and committed to leading by example
but still having to turn the other cheek
for the woman that's faced her fears in her career
but still too afraid to love out loud
for the woman that has been scarred by love
but loves any way

I write for her
she's been quiet for too long
aching to be heard for too long
I write because
If I don't
she won't
make it
I speak it
her truth
because I am her too

I write for She
she be tired
but strong

She be exhausted
  but stoic
    Resilient but lacks the strength to say I'm
tired

I write for you
I promise I never forget about you

I write for us

Those Little Eyes

The cornea helps your eye focus light so you can see clearly.
Much like a window to the soul,
it controls and focuses the entry of light into the eye;
Refracts the light,
bends the light,
Limits the amount of light that shines too bright into the eye.

Tunnel vision.

The loss of peripheral sight.
Objects are only seen in the center of the visual field

They used to only see my greatness.
Standing atop my exalted pedestal,
I stood
statuesque
in all of my perfect parental glory
A beauty to be held in those little eyes.
Untainted
Unblemished
They saw protection.

They saw mommy.
They saw no wrong.
All the Crocked roads I’ve walked
didn't mean anything in those eyes

Corneal abrasion, resulting in
Blurry vision
Red eyes
Watery eyes
Sensitivity to light

They became teenagers and those little eyes
didn't see me the same anymore

they were hungrily searching for their own
identity
they wanted a taste of freedom
wanted to lick the spoon of adulthood
they starting kicking and screaming and knocked
me off my pedestal
their peripheral vision became clear
they loaded their artillery with my flaws of mass
destruction and the communication skills i
taught them as a defense mechanism
they studied the art of war
I became target for their hatred
because they couldn't see me anymore

when your cornea is damaged

your vision becomes opaque and hazy
There's a glare now
Where the light was clear
When they stare at me
There's no halo now
No angel
No majestic mythical creature
That kept them safe from danger
the opinions of their peers is their virtual reality
I'm only 3D
I could see farther than their eyes could adjust to
but my viewpoint limited

I've learned that the most critical eyes
belong to the people you've created
eventually they find a way to humanize you
the blinders come off and they no longer idealize you
they only see you through their corneal abrasion
blurry, unclear, unsure

the cornea is the fastest healing tissue of the body;
healing itself in less than 36 hours
it's been years now
it appears the damage may be permanent
i wonder if my kids will ever see ME
again…through those little eyes

My Truth

I’m insecure at times
I don't know if you can tell
I heard that I cover it up real well
but there are times when I doubt me

I’m a poet
A writer
A spoken word artist
I say “late bloomer”
  some say right on time
I be thinking that I’m too old to start performing
now
they be like
  nah.
they tell me how my poetry moves them
  and I find a way to diminish how great I am
play small
  be modest
    tell them "Thank you so much!"
as if I didn’t know
  my work is solid gold
I crawled through disappointment, trauma and
tragedy
  just so i can put pen to paper
    to caution those that come after me

I’m somebody’s mama
I created people
not alone
  but I’m the only one that stayed behind to do
the raising
It’s crazy
  how I be more concerned about their daddy
coming
    to steal my glory after all the years I spent
      beaten from the stormy weather of
parenting
rather than
  how his absence translates to adult therapy for
them
I'm selfish
  it's about them
    but not really
i knew him before they did
  he did me wrong first
I’m due an apology

I’m a wife
on my worst days he loves at me his best
my past experience with toxic relationships
  sits in a little rocking chair in the left corner of
my mind
    twiddling it's thumbs
asking me if I'm gonna go through his phone

check his emails for trails of infidelity
all while his love for me and my respect for him
is wrapped around my neck
suffocating the old life out of me
blowing shotguns of reassurance into my
breath
on my worst days he loves me at his best

I'm a businesswoman
with a business I don't know how to run
somehow it provides the next dollar
when I don't know
where the next dollar is coming from
4 out of 7days I move like a monster mogul
stop and grab a fancy cup of coffee
check my calendar for meetings
drive around Houston to determine
what neighborhood I want to buy my first
house in
and those other 3 days
my laziness takes over
my ego is smothered by all the things I don't
know
all the things that I have to learn
in order for my business to grow
I feel like I'm kinda old
my brain feels like it moves kinda slow

I'm insecure at times

I don't know if you can tell
I heard that I cover it up real well
but there are times when I doubt me

I straddle the fence between self doubt and confidence
Imposter syndrome
possibly

I Woke Up This Morning

I woke up this morning
Grateful that I made it through the night and I get to see another day that the Lord has made

Took a deep breath and let rest return to my lungs
Stretched my limbs, twisted my body in all kinds of positions
-exhaled the stiffness away

I woke up this morning
Let the excitement of what joy the day holds for me wash over my weary body
and refill my spirit from yesterday's depletion

I cried tears filled with gratitude that I don't look like what I been through
and that my faith ain't shattered due to the disappointments I've been going
through
and that life ain't always easy but you live to see it through

i woke up this morning
Did a praise break in my spirit

Told my creator "I surrender"
  I surrender
    every day to your will and your way
I sing praises unto your name
  so everyone will hear me say...
He kept me

I woke up this morning

Home

I was born in Queens, New York.
I was raised in West Palm Beach, Florida.
I come from a Jamaican woman and an
American man that couldn't figure out whether
they loved each other enough to stay together.
So we bounced.
Bounced from the bottom of the US to the top
and stopped several times in between.
I've seen the map of the US a thousand times
and I still don't know where home is.

Brooklyn.

Brooklyn is where adulthood crept in and
lassoed me into responsibility.
Weekday mornings spent subway surfing with
my coffee in my left hand,
brass knuckles in the right, my feet firmly
planted on the train floor ready to take off into
the to the city that never sleeps.
The sound of my feet hitting the pavement
favoring the heartbeat of the city that never
sleeps. The sound of my weariness escapes

when I breathe. I'm exhausted in the city that never sleeps 'cause I ain't been to sleep either.

I was tired. So I left. Collected my kids like miscellaneous clothes thrown into duffel bags. Chucked the deuce and made my feet move like I knew what I was doing but honestly I had no clue. I knew, in my world, roses never grew from concrete -only weeds and vines crept up the sides of brick walls and brownstones so I slipped my Tims on and hit the ground running. Slathered the petroleum jelly under my eyes, made my cheeks slippery enough to let the blows glide over my skin without swelling my eyes.
I cried my eyes shut when I left because I knew I'd turn to salt if I ever looked back.

Injustice Peace

It’s not fair that the words that you speak wreak of privilege
  - that your mouth can spew out compilations of words like “I don’t see color”
The audacity of you to disregard my hue until it’s time to approve my home loan
  - that’s when my color shines brighter than your red pen as you outline
    sections on the map forcing me to stay in my zone
      keeping all the blacks on the other side of the tracks
"We’ll give them parks and schools but the taxes they pay won’t be enough to lift them out of their current tax bracket"

Gentrified hoods be the distraction to keep the masses distracted from the truth
  while they spoon feed our culture to the masses
Snatch our edges
  body parts
    slang
      music
        art

then appropriate
So the culture rises up outta the ghetto but the people can’t

Teenagers

You are a child.
Over stimulated raging teenage hormones.
You reek of insubordination.
2 horns form at the outer points of your doom.
Fangs at your canines
  you spit venom through those baby teeth.
Speak with indignation.
Your vocabulary be that of an average high schooler
  yet you manage to crochet Insults, flipped birds, and curse words into a
    blanket of mutiny as if you've been here before.
You lack respect for authority
  yet,
    I love you still.

Love

I've been pushing my mind to see this body
differently.
To see the blemishes as glitter…
bling…
a little razzle dazzle.
To see the lines in my skin as pathways to self
discovery.
A journey
to love me
more

Pride - Part 1

There were moments I diminished her feelings
Told her she was going through a phase
Told her she won't always feel this way
Told her how girls have sex -
  not as a way to teach her
but as a way to deter her from wanting the
physical experience
I made it sound unappealing
  intentionally
So She hid from me
  for a long time

Aging

I see the wrinkles forming around the corners of my mouth.
I wonder if I continue my fight against time will I tire out before the last round.
Did I have children too early and in the process of learning how to be a mother I forgot to nurture myself?
Did I wait too long to put my dreams on a pedestal?
All of my desires placed on pause
  -placed on a shelf far from my reach
Is it too late for me to reach for the stars?
Is it too dark at night to see wisdom?
Is it too bright during the day to see my truth?
Aging is like a shadow, it follows whether you want it to or not.

Accolades

Where does your mind wander to when the
applause stops?
When you're standing on stage. No back drop.
No props.
No curtains to pull back
And you're convinced the audience forgot
Forgot that their standing ovation pumps blood
through your body
That their accolades gives way to your creativity
Ironically, that's not their responsibility,
That doesn't mean that you don't live for it.
That you don't enjoy it.
That you don't strive for it.
That you don't get high off of it .
It doesn't mean that I don't feign for it,
that my ego don't geek for it,
that I tried to stay clean from it
but when I close my eyes and see pitch black
my ears still want more of it.
I want an encore for my encore.
It's my drug of choice.
Sometimes I follow the rule
of never get high on your own supply
so me rooting for myself don't come easy all the
time.

I’m human.
And standing here in this moment telling you what I go through
before I choose to disclose my woes
makes me more vulnerable than my opponent.
And since I’ve been hiding this notion for some time now
I really don’t care who knows it.
These are valid emotions I’m disclosing.

When the silence hits and ain’t nobody checking for me
my ego be bruised but not broken,
but I be wanting to be wanted.
The validation ain’t needed, it’s wanted.
The comradery ain’t needed, it’s wanted.
The ferocious explosion of social promotion ain’t needed, it’s wanted.
That’s why my words are spoken out loud
in front of crowds that appear distorted
from this side of the stage.
I can’t explain why I am this way
what I can say is I’m honest,
and that’s most important .

Who doesn't want to be revered by their peers?
Let’s say you post your original content on social media and only get 11 shares,
Some might say, "OK, today was a good day!"

Others might feel like nobody cares.
I am others.
I got 14 first cousins and 2 brothers,
I need for them to share 10 times over plus one extra for good measure.
This request ain't something I'm not willing to offer
I know that your show of admiration is what is catapulting me to my purpose
so remember that every time you clap for an artist
they become more determined to show you they're worth it.
I know it's challenging to stand in your truth
and admit that, you too, live for this-
and I ain't trying to convince you to make some type of announcement
cause that's your business.
I acknowledge my plight because it makes me feel fearless.
I'm just saying, there's time when the yearning for acceptance feels like a prison
and I crash into the barb-wired fence with a quickness
when there's too much stillness.
But I still write though,
and I still perform though.
Even when the crowd stops clapping
Imma keep going till my eyes close,

cause only God knows what I would go through
if I didn’t have a show to go to.

Women

standing in the bank
waiting for the bank teller
to acknowledge me
no rush
i sneeze
i bleed
i feel the blood from my cycle gather in my
panties
almost ready to run down my leg
it's that time of the month again.

standing in the grocery store
leaning over the tomatoes
i lift one to my nose
a woman and her baby strolls by
our eyes say hi
baby cries
my shirt, wet,
nipples, erect
that ain't even my baby
my nursing breasts don't know the difference.

standing in the mall
unable to decide which mall hallway will grab
my eye

i notice a mother in panic
she can't find her toddler
"she was just standing right here"
i sensed her fear
it travels from her to me
now i can't breath
she can't find her baby
but i'm the one crying.

standing in the bathroom
i'm angry
he lied to me again and the other woman is here
too
the lady in blue walks through the door
she greets me "You ok, Queen?"
my eyelids fill with tears and she catches them
i weep in her arms
i never met her before.

standing in the mirror
evaluating my physical self
it's Wednesday
i feel good today
my wrinkles and stretch marks
aren't as prominent and my smile doesn't feel
forced
my belly feels like love today
today I'm a snack.

My Heart

The doctor said the very thing that's killing me
is keeping me alive.

I said you don't get to decide if my eyes close at
the end of this line.

The doctor said my heart is fighting against my
will to live.

I said even if my heart doesn't beat as easily the
will in me is greater
And my diagnosis does not define me.
There's no bucket list of things to accomplish,
No must do's or must have's
I simply jump out of my bed, stand ten toes
down, make direct eye contact with forever and
say "Today is gonna be better than yesterday!"
There's no doctor that can convince me that each
chamber of my heart ain't filled to the brim with
the passion for life my creator gave me

I'm following my soul on this journey of
discovering my purpose
And the God I know promised me it would be
worth it,

so I slap fives in his name with every milestone reached.
Scream out loud in appreciation when my lungs expand to their fullest capacity.
Let the tears stream down my cheeks and form puddles of gratitude at my feet
because even though tomorrow ain't guaranteed to me
it's my responsibility to be a beacon of light for every man, woman, and child, that experiences me.

I am every breath he takes.
I am every wink of her eye.
I am every click of my ancestor's tongue.
I am love wrapped in joy,
simmered in peace,
standing in truth right before you.
I am life.

Hardheaded

Sometimes I gotta remind myself
that their decisions are not mine.
Whether they fail or prevail it's still theirs
and I dare not wear the consequences of their
decisions.
When they don't listen it feels like incisions in
my heart.
A 2 inch slit in my right chamber where all my
blood enters but seeps out because my children
don't listen
To logic
Or Rationality

I want to be loved

Take me as i am
With every flaw that i care not to point out
but will because you deserve knowing
what you're walking into

You get to choose if this mayhem
will fit into your puzzle
Will we click like legos
or will you let go because
letting go is easier

Will you let my love adorn you
in the crevices of your fractured heart
The parts where love may have skipped over
unintentionally
Can I be the magnet that draws your
fragmented pieces into a new creation

Can i be your inspiration
Hold my hand
interlock fingers
and jump off of this bridge with me
knowing that I'm not perfect, nor do I aspire to
be
But I am complete

and once we jump
everything behind us becomes irrelevant

Millennial Friends

My friend went to the doctor
she wasn't feeling well lately
and it became necessary to take a mental health day
she couldn't bear to see the sun come out some days
the twinkle in her babies' eyes didn't gleam the same way
body don't mean much some days
so, she neglected it
soap against her skin felt like needles and pins
toothbrushes looked like daggers aimed at her gums
she said she wanted to run
from life and I was like…
Why?

she began to peel back layers of her mind like notebook pages
pages after pages
of phases of life that felt so unfair
I started to believe that she was made of vibranium
built different

tough
indestructible
solid
energy bigger than a boulder
I wondered how she did it
how did she live outside of herself so well?
she said it was the pebbles
the little things
all the sticks and stones that broke everyone
else's bones
only strengthened hers
she built towers out of fake smiles and hidden
cries
tucked her sadness into lies like
"It's ok".
"It's no big deal"
"I don't mind"

Whole time she'd be running through brick
walls
trying to fight her way out of her own thoughts
maze runner

Running after her sanity
trying to catch a flight just to get high
just to get by
haze runner

running away from the slightest possibility

of becoming her mama
track runner

I couldn't imagine my insides fluctuating like
this
she said been living her whole life like this
A mixture of adolescent dreams and adult
screams
the gift and the curse of empathy
She told me a story about when she was 6
I know I paid attention but
I don't know if I blocked it out of my memory
or I just couldn't believe it enough to repeat it

My friend be struggling
and sometimes I don't know when
because we're grown women and
we're millennials so we're respecting boundaries
and allowing our friends to live freely
but I be too scared to let her swim past the bouys
afraid she might get sucked under a tsunami of
thoughts
and drown in her rage
I am afraid to let my friend drift off into the deep
end
afraid to let her wade in the waters knowing that
If I blink too fast, I'll lose her

Black Dick

Black Dick
Melanin rich
Thick
Beautiful
Black
Girthy and fun
And it stands at attention
Projecting its magnificent silhouette against the majestic backdrop that is his skin

Black dick
Knocks down walls
And fills up dark spaces
Leaves traces of black lacquer
Against your lips

Black dick
The catalyst to the creation of melanated nations
The fertilization of black embryos
Also curled toes

Black dick
Solution oriented
Problems dissolve once inserted

We should award it
The noble peace prize
Because butterflies rise in bellies
When it's full potential is realized

Black dick
Leaves minds hypnotized
Immobilized
When eyes stretch wide to observe it's full size

Black dick
Pussies cum quick for you
Pussies thump hard for you
Ooze love, lust, desire, and pussy juice for you
Breathing speeds up for you
Inhibitions to the wind
"Im just gon' lick the tip since I don't normally do this" for you

Black dick
You stimulate orgasmic power
Power play your massive shaft into my happy place
Have my ancestral love tribal dancing
To the beat of your djembe drum

Black dick.

Moving On

I had to leave him behind
forget the life we shared
the life we created in our youth
i had to move on without him
so that my new life wouldn't
get caught in the loop

Isaac (Ode to Fashion Designer Isaac Moore)

She laughed in the face of God
when promised that the grandfather of many nations
will be born from her barren womb

The son of Abraham brought forth the vision
of a great nation and God's promise and purpose was fixed
for all those who descended from him

Isaac.
The miracle child.
Spared by God in the last moment.
The father of Esau and Jacob.
From his loins came the 12 tribes of Israel.
With faith and obedience what more is required?

A vision.
A determination to remain consistent in the face of adversity.
A vision.
To be black excellence with every stitch and flick of the wrist.
A vision.

To be evolution in style while kicking down
every door that slammed.
There's no need for handouts.
A vision
To create a future,
not designed by circumstance,
but by survival of the fittest.
You must step outside of the box to live this
experience.
It is not for the weak.
So when they tell you no,
be prepared to redesign your life.

www.ingramcontent.com/pod-product-compliance
Lightning Source LLC
Chambersburg PA
CBHW051746130826
49812CB00033B/1024
* 9 7 8 9 3 5 7 2 1 0 5 5 3 *